A CONCOCTION OF THOUGHTS

AYUSH SAXENA

To my mother and father
Arti Saxena and Nitin Saxena

Contents

Contents

Preface

The idea to write this book was in my mind for the past few months, I thought it would be great to make a book just out of motivational quotes related to problems we face in current society and also some inspirational poems which are light reads & make you feel good about yourself, just like a self-care medicine and make you remember greatest moments with your loved Ones and give you strength and enthusiasm to create more such moments to remember. In relation to what we have faced as a society in the past 2 years (Covid-19) it has made us realize how uncertain life is, thus I wanted to write something that makes us value our lives more and do whatever we want to, right now. As I am a student, publishing my own book with a reputed publishing house was a huge challenge for me, but the "Poetic Souls" publication gave me an opportunity to do this through their "Daily Scribblings 4.0" program, Hence I invite you to take a dive into a sea of motivation and experiences as you read this book, if reading it brings a smile on your face I would think I accomplished my goal, have a great time reading it.....

Acknowledgements

Writing a book requires a lot of motivation, inspiration, and help thus I want to express my gratitude to each and everyone who supported me from the start of this journey, first and foremost I would like to thank everyone from the publishing team. I express my humble gratitude to everyone on the "Poetic souls publications team" who helped me so much from the start. Thank you for providing me an opportunity to write my own book through an incredible initiative like "Daily Scribblings 4.0", moving forward I want to thank my parents for inspiring and keeping me motivated throughout the process, and my younger brother for being my youngest critic and bringing in a different perspective, I want to thank fellow members of the writing community who helped me throughout the process in writing my first book, and finally, I want to thank the almighty for all that I've been blessed with, hope you enjoy this book as a read which makes you revisit some of the greatest experiences of your life.

About The Author

Ayush Saxena is an engineer who completed his engineering from SRM University, Chennai, and he is also an award-winning writer who has contributed to more than 8 anthologies with his poems and motivational quotes, for which he was awarded the "Master of rhymes award" which was followed by many more achievements in the field of writing. He lives in the city of lakes Bhopal, M.P. He started his journey of writing on Instagram last year on his page "Poemsopedia" under the name of " Arnit " inspired by his parents "Arti and Nitin saxena", He was able to attract followers as well as some great members of the writing community through his works, He takes inspiration from the most ordinary incidences in daily life, nature, and abstract topics making his writings immensely relatable and sometimes making you remember similar experiences, Through his writings, he aims to make the reader relive beautiful experiences of his/her life and aims to bring a smile on the reader's face.

ONE

POET THAT PENNED LIFE DOWN

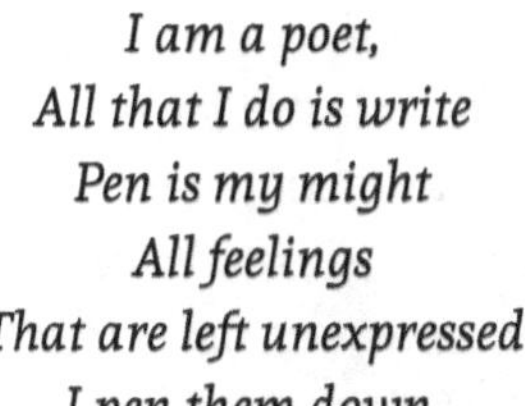

I am a poet,
All that I do is write
Pen is my might
All feelings
That are left unexpressed
I pen them down.

The first smile of a baby
So pure and serene
No mother can describe
The delight her eyes see
But still I am just a poet
All I did was penned it down

The first steps of a toddler
Denote a new beginning
towards the future

A CONCOCTION OF THOUGHTS

A father witnesses his future
Walking on its own footsteps
Which he with love has nurtured
But still I am just a poet, i just witnessed
All i did was penned it down

The days of school, The days of results
Endless excitement frolic and fun
Mum's Scolding for the homework
Dad's love for the endless demands
Parents witnessing
Dreams of future growing up
But still I am just a poet
All i did was penned it down

I saw many such events in my life
Experienced some of them myself
But sadly it lasted for not very long
Thus I found a solution,
For everyone to experience this delight
I am a poet, and proudly
I penned it down ....

TWO
CHILDHOOD FORGOTTEN

I've forgotten my Childhood,
But it still echoes in my heart
I've forgotten how days passed
But I still remember that lap,
In which i slept in utmost comfort
Carefree, even in sleep I laughed.

I've forgotten how I touched the skies,
But I still remember those sturdy shoulders,
which carried me when i cried
All I thought was that I could touch the skies
But with those shoulders supporting me i learnt how to fly.

I've forgotten those shaky fingers,
But I still remember,
They held me tight whenever I stumbled
I've forgotten those eyes, watching over me through spectacles

But I still remember ,
I watched the world through their vision

I've forgotten the scolding I got
I've forgotten the mischief i did
But i still remember the lessons I learnt
I still remember the endless fun
I still remember the smiles I earned

Sadly I've forgotten most of my childhood
As many of you might have,
But I still remember
At heart I am the same child i was then

Love those who are with you today
Love those who you lost on the way
As you are a piece of them,
You might have forgotten your childhood
But you still remember traces of them
As you've parts of your childhood
alive inside you even today

THREE

THE FERRY THAT LOST ITS WAY

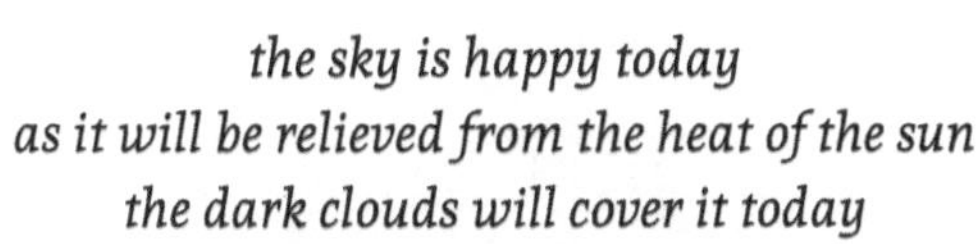

the sky is happy today
as it will be relieved from the heat of the sun
the dark clouds will cover it today
to make its day calm and cool
and let it loosen up.

the raindrops are eager to fall
they are eager to huddle
all they wish to see is
a sight of children playing in the puddle
all they want to carry
is a small and lovely paper ferry.

but today the raindrops will not fall
as the sight which they wanted to witness is lost
the children they played with are gone
they've lost interest in their puddles
and with their phones, they've formed a new huddle

A CONCOCTION OF THOUGHTS

I still wish for the rain to come
to gently remind them of the fun
to be united once again
to be dirty and happy again
I wish the puddles return soon
so that I can take the last ride,
on that paper ferry too...

FOUR

REMEMBERING CHILDHOOD

In the room of life ,
There's still a bright corner
Childhood is kept there,
Once again in those memories
I want to lose myself somewhere,
I want those days back
when there was only school bag
That seemed heavy,
With growing up and giving it up,
The life seems way more heavy
I wish those times can be relived someday,
When we slept on floor
And woke up on the bed next day
I hope everyone's life is full of light,
But I still wish
that corner of childhood remains forever bright....

FIVE

LIFE IS SHORT

Life is short, be happy in everything...
Be happy in the voice of the face that is not near you...
If someone is angry with you, be happy in their style of anger...
Be happy in remembrance of those who will not come back.
Those Who have Witnessed yesterday...
Be happy in your today...
As it will not Come back

SIX

SOMETIME BE WITH YOURSELF

It is good to spend time with yourself,
it is good if you introduce yourself to your inner self...

It is better than walking in the crowd with the world,
That you go for a walk with yourself.

It is better if you light a lamp inside yourself.....
Than To Walk in the light of the lamp lit-up by Someone else..

Rather than being a person of pure thoughts
It is better to be true to yourself.

You have travelled all over the world, now it is good if you come
back to yourself.

Rather than Sitting silently in loneliness,
It's better if you sing your own melodies
To yourself

SEVEN

LEAVE

"Just walk in awe on the fallen dry leaves.

For Once you had sought shelter from them in the harsh sun."

EIGHT

I CAN'T CRY

I have tears in my eyes... but I can't cry.
people taunt people laugh at me, but
I can't bear the burden of taunts now
I have tears in my eyes but I can't Cry

Hopes are attached to me,
Endless journey of life is yet to complete
when I reached home i Promised that no matter how difficult it
might be,
i Can't lose self-confidence
I have tears in my eyes But I can't Cry

If there are dark clouds of sorrow, and there are storms of
difficulties,
I can't have tears in my eyes
I will show you the winning bet
I will reach my destination one day no matter what the path
is, without reaching the destination, I can't sleep
I have tears in my eyes but I can't cry.

NINE

LEARNINGS FROM LIFE

An injury to the foot teaches us to walk carefully and an injury to the mind teaches us to live wisely, so never be afraid of injuries as they are learnings in disguise.

TEN

SIGHT

Sight is an eternal gift
We witness the world through it
It is a window which lets us see
The world which lies outside
Our mind and our feels
But it has an another perspective
Our sight is very reflective
It offers the view that we often ignore
It offers a reflection of our soul
Nobody can see what lies inside one's mind
But the sight can introspect inner depths of one's mind
The best sight isn't the one
Which offers sceneries of hills and beaches
But the one which gives
True view of people's inner selves.

ELEVEN

BURDENS

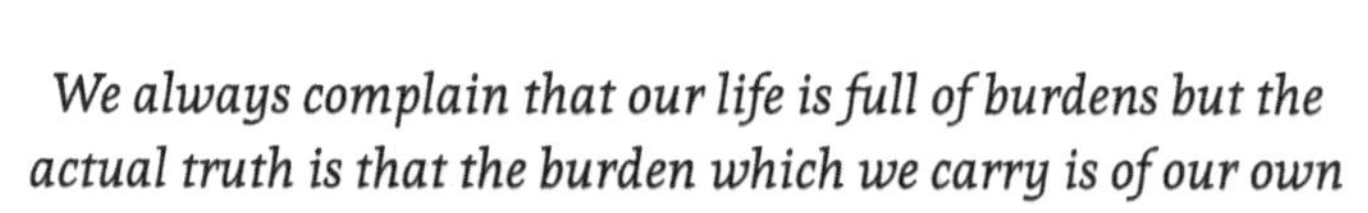

We always complain that our life is full of burdens but the actual truth is that the burden which we carry is of our own expectations and desires. if we drop some off our back, then the life will be light and easy.

TWELVE
LIGHT OF LIFE

Life is an opportunity to absorb what is good, reflect what inspires,
refract the evil and to emit positivity.

THIRTEEN

I'LL TAKE CARE

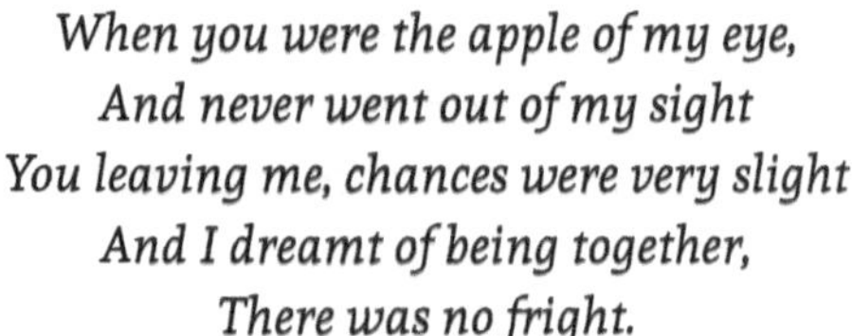

When you were the apple of my eye,
And never went out of my sight
You leaving me, chances were very slight
And I dreamt of being together,
There was no fright.

I thought this would last forever
I thought you would only be mine
Till the world ends,
You'll be on my side,
But it wasn't meant to be the same
As you left , my fears came true
I became aware of truth of life
We weren't meant to be forever
But don't worry, I'll take care.

Your memories will remain with me forever
My hope will never be lost, as I want to be together
Yet if you return, ever
Don't be sympathetic as , I'll take care.

FOURTEEN

TIME NEVER STOPS

Time does not have enough time to stop and give you time again to make up for the lost time.

FIFTEEN

TRAVELLER

Man is a traveller, he comes & goes
While traveling leaves memories & sorrows
A gust of wind, in heavy downpours
He lives in crowd, but still is alone
Left alone to mourn on his loneliness
Man is a traveller, he comes & goes
While traveling he leaves trails of tears
Which were of pain amd fear
Stranded in a bad nightmare
no escape found near
Heart trembles soul shivers,
Shaky bones everyone can here
Man is a traveller, he comes & goes
While traveling towards the light of hope.

SIXTEEN

TEACHINGS FROM LIFE

Life teaches a lot, sometimes it makes you laugh, sometimes makes you cry, but life bows its head in front of those who live without expectations and are happy in every situation.

SEVENTEEN
LOST AND FOUND

I enjoyed wandering,
When I was lost
I roamed around aimlessly
When I was lost
Carefree and aloof i was
When I was lost
Responsibility was just a vague word
When I was lost
Credibility was not a friend of mine
When I was lost
Happiness in life was a mirage
When I was lost
Realisation hit harder than ever
When I actually lost myself
The blindfold of carefree world untied
Eyes witnessed truth of life
I lost my senses, yet i realised
Life doesn't always gives you what you like,
Hence, I collected shattered parts of mine,
Joined them to make a glass
A glass that only showed truth,

AYUSH SAXENA

When asked what changed my inner self,
I just answered,
I found myself......

EIGHTEEN

LOST

Lost I was ,
but still I was happy,
as i was living a mirage as my dream,
but when I came out of it,
the dream ended,
reality found me,
but when I found my real self,
I realised that
I actually lost
from my inner self.

NINETEEN

LIFE A POND TO PONDER

Life is like a pond of clear water
Which ripples when stones of difficulties collide with it,
Which smiles back to you, when you look towards it and smile,
Which reflects your deeds as they are
Which flows when gentle wind of happiness passes through
Which dries up when heat of stress rises
So life is a pond of clear water,
It reflects what you do,
It becomes what you want it to be.

TWENTY
WHAT TO DO

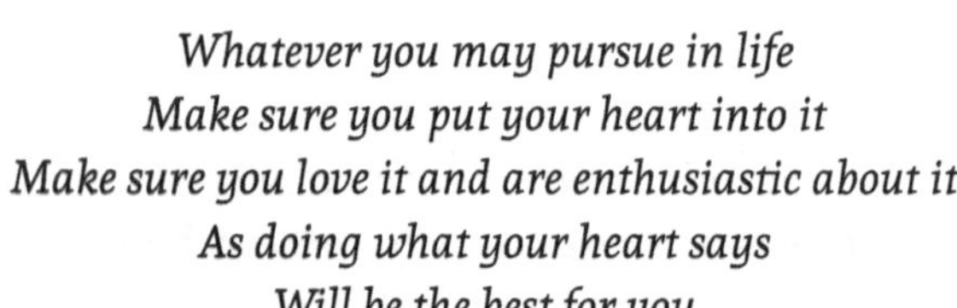

Whatever you may pursue in life
Make sure you put your heart into it
Make sure you love it and are enthusiastic about it
As doing what your heart says
Will be the best for you
And will never leave you feeling detached...

TWENTY-ONE

HEART AN EMPTY BASKET

Heart is not a basket to keep stress and apathy..!
It is a golden vessel to have happiness and sweet memories....!!

TWENTY-TWO
KEEP GOING

We are nomads in this land of life,
we travel from the brightest days
To the darkest nights,
But yet we have to continue our journey
So, don't be disheartened and upset
Don't be dim, as the sky in the evenings
Life has a new morning every day,
Keep rising as the sun,
And shine in your own rays

TWENTY-THREE
SISTER'S AFFECTION

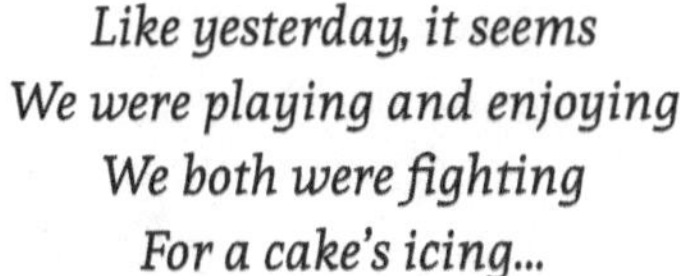

Like yesterday, it seems
We were playing and enjoying
We both were fighting
For a cake's icing...

Like yesterday, it seems
We were in our teens
We enjoyed pulling
Each other's leg,
Sometimes it was
quite a long stretch

Yesterday is past, now.
Present has finally approached
As I watch you standing there,
I'm shedding bittersweet tears.
But I know that

A CONCOCTION OF THOUGHTS

You'll be fine there,

But still it makes me sad
I'll never forget our chats.
And your daily rants
Hope you will still be with me
And will buy me a gift
whenever we meet

Now, you're going that's alright,
New responsibilities,a new life
But this is not the end, I know
there are many more chats to go

I will miss you seldom,
As your Lier brother
As you know
Wherever future might take us
You'll always be my sister,

TWENTY-FOUR

MIRRORS STAND STILL

In this world of fading memories
It is necessary to take some photos
In the remembrance of those beautiful moments,
As truth is mirrors do not show what passed away they always
show the reality the present....

TWENTY-FIVE
PATH OF LIFE

When you don't get a chance to think about how enjoyable the destination would be, while walking on the path to it, you should know that you are on the right track. Goal will surely satisfy your mind but the journey you travelled to achieve it will satisfy your soul.

TWENTY-SIX
BAD TIMES ARE SHORT LIVED

Keep doing the right thing and be patient Don't give up
on yourself,
Never back down,
Hopes might be lost,
But never let your head down,
Bad times may hurt you a lot
but remember to stand your ground
because someday bad times will also have bad times...

TWENTY-SEVEN
TRUE FRIEND

A friend is the one who is sitting nearby even if there is no chatter going on.
And still you feel secure and happy that he is sitting nearby.
A friend's presence is like magic
It makes you feel happy and energetic
Even when you don't understand the logic behind it

TWENTY-EIGHT
STEPS

I don't want everything I desire at once, I just want that my next step
Towards what I desire should be better than the last one

TWENTY-NINE
CRITICISM

"Criticism" is a part and parcel of journey towards your target
But don't get bewildered if you receive it,
and lose path to your "target", because as soon as you achieve
your "target",
the "View" of critics will change.

THIRTY
FOG

There is only enough power in the fog to 'blur the way towards your dream'
There is no such fog that can make you lose sight of your dream, of your goal 'of your destination'.

THIRTY-ONE
TEARS TO HAPPINESS

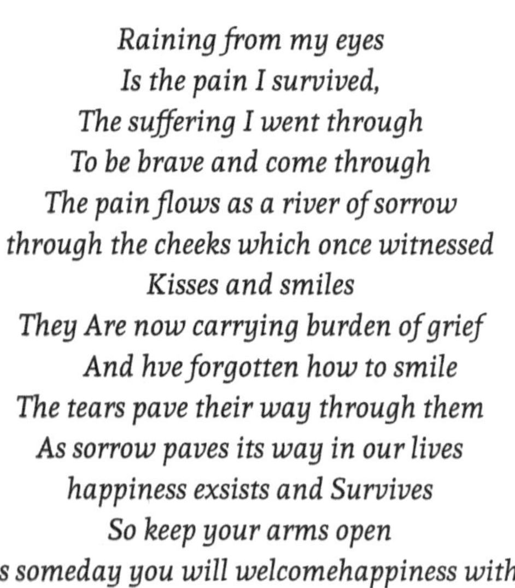

Raining from my eyes
Is the pain I survived,
The suffering I went through
To be brave and come through
The pain flows as a river of sorrow
through the cheeks which once witnessed
Kisses and smiles
They Are now carrying burden of grief
And hve forgotten how to smile
The tears pave their way through them
As sorrow paves its way in our lives
happiness exsists and Survives
So keep your arms open
As someday you will welcomehappiness with
Lots of hugs......

THIRTY-TWO
GOAL & DREAM

There is only one difference between a dream and a goal, dreams require effortless sleep and to achieve a goal, sleepless effort is required....

THIRTY-THREE
LIFE

In life, smile as you have a pocket full of sunshine, The sun sets and rises again, As it knows without it life in this world a will not be possible, as is living a life without smile, it is impossible...

THIRTY-FOUR
INTENT

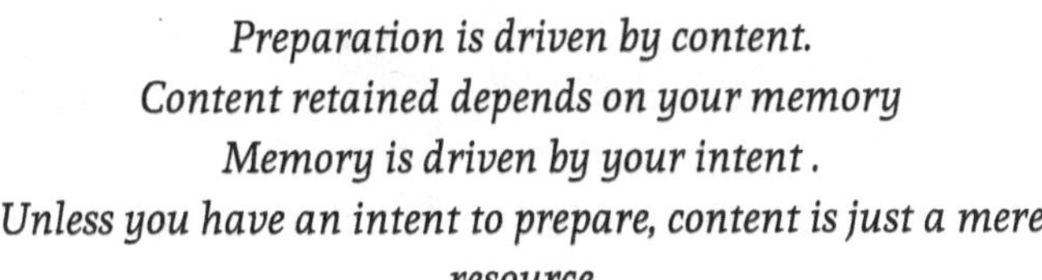

Preparation is driven by content.
Content retained depends on your memory
Memory is driven by your intent .
Unless you have an intent to prepare, content is just a mere
resource

THIRTY-FIVE
CHANGE

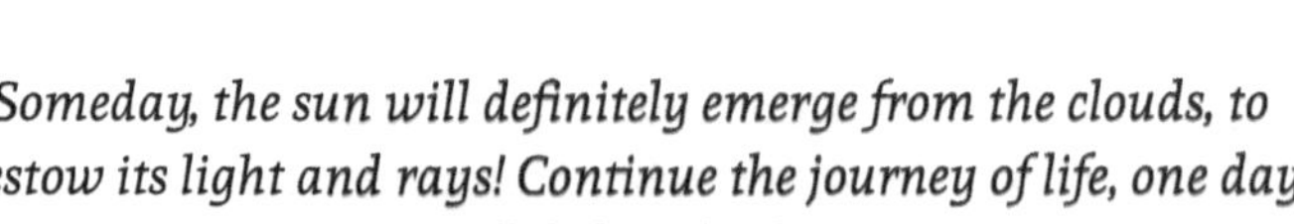

Someday, the sun will definitely emerge from the clouds, to bestow its light and rays! Continue the journey of life, one day time will definitely change !!
As nothing in this world is permanent..

THIRTY-SIX
STAY, LIGHT OF HOPE

Stay with me the light of hope
as the sun has not set yet
Don't hurry some dreams & goals
Are yet to be met,
Many unsaid words still wait,
They wait for you to come,
Stay so they can illuminate
The seeds of thoughts,
Haven't grown yet,
Stay with me and let them germinate
Never leave me behind,
As on you I depend,
My light of hope be my companion
As with your hope my life's journey
Will attain its purpose
The goals which I set
The dreams which I dreamt.....

THIRTY-SEVEN
VALUES OF LIFE

Who is the "intelligent"
The one who "learns" the most
Who is "powerful"
The one who has control over "desires"
Who is "humble"
The one who is "kind" to others
Who is "honoured"
The One who "respects" others,
Who is free from "hatred"
The one who "loves" others
who is "wealthy"
The one who has "love & care" of family
What are "values"
They're the reflection of your "brought up"
Who is "full of life"
The one who has "values" and values others.

THIRTY-EIGHT

IN PURSUIT OF HAPPINESS

My heart is searching again
Those days of leisure,
When my life didn't gave me pain.
Those days of laughter,
Those days of happiness,
Which i lost somewhere ,
Now my heart is searching for those days again.

Hope i will find them dropped somewhere on the way,
Waiting for me to arrive,
As i will pick them again
This time I'll treasure them
I'll keep them close to my heart
As life is incomplete without moments
Moments of laughter
Moments of happiness.
And the kept experiences of the past

THIRTY-NINE
RELATIONS

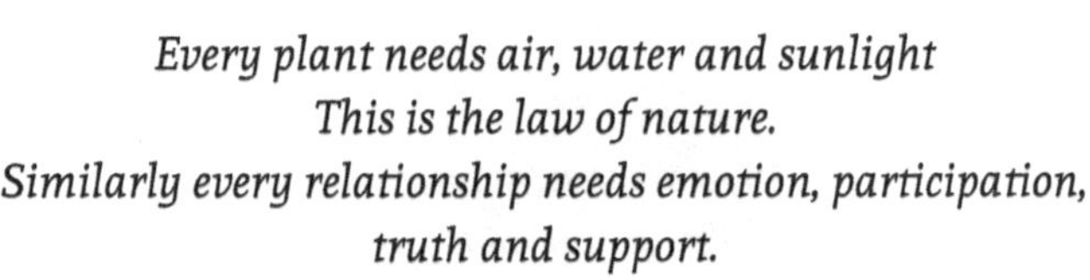

Every plant needs air, water and sunlight
This is the law of nature.
Similarly every relationship needs emotion, participation,
truth and support.
To grow stronger and to flourish.

FORTY

FRIENDSHIP

Friendship is like hands and eyes because,
When your hand gets hurt,
Tears come out from the eyes,
and when tears come out from the eyes, only hands come up to
wipe them.

About Poetic Souls

Poetic Souls is writer's community, where we grow together while helping each other.
Motivation and ideas are what we all seek and give.
Prompts, Challenges and various activities help a writer to think beyond the box and helps in their overall development.
Apart from this we also provide an author platform which encourages budding writer's to enhance their skills and make their work, reach a target audience of potential readers. ...
Its a growing community of the writers, managed by Rohan Nath and Nidhi Shukla.